Grandma Kitty's Coloring Book of Poetry

Copyright © 2022 by Kitty Kaye

Illustrations copyright © 2022 by Debbe Femiak

All rights reserved

Table of Contents

<u>Verses for Children</u> 5
Believe in Yourself 7
Beautiful You 9
A Good Friend 11
Forgiven 13
Grow in Grace 15
Let's Be Silly 17
Upside Down Frown 19

<u>Words of Comfort</u> 21
Hold On 23
Lead Me, Lord 25
Rebuilding 27
The Storm 29
Trusting God 31

Verses for Children

<u>Believe in Yourself</u>

*Believe in yourself-
There's so much more to you.
You have lots of talent,
and gifts that will shine through.*

*You were made to thrive,
so special and so smart.
You've got a lot to offer
by following your heart.*

*Discover what you're good at,
the things that you enjoy.
Then focus on those talents,
and fill the world with joy.*

*Don't ever be discouraged,
Never, ever give up,
Until you have achieved your goal
and filled the world with love.*

*So let this be a lesson
to you my little elf-
Make the world a better place
by believing in yourself.*

<u>*Beautiful You*</u>

*Beautiful you-
So lovely, so sweet.
A spirit like yours
Just cannot be beat.*

*Your eyes, how they sparkle
Your smile, how it shines.
Your laughter, delightful-
Brings peace to my mind.*

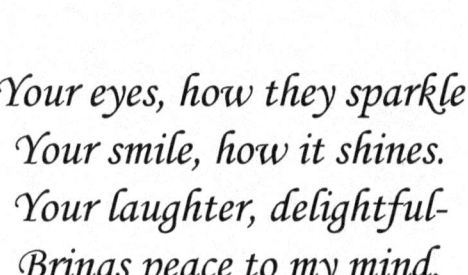

*Your words are so clever,
So cute and so smart.
The things that you say
Bring joy to my heart.*

*Your life makes me happy,
Your soul makes mine sing.
And if up to me, well-
I wouldn't change a thing.*

*Be strong and be proud,
Enjoy who you are.
Because you, my friend,
Are a bright, shining star.*

A Good Friend

Smile, my friend -
Be happy, be good.
Share your love,
your toys, your food.

Be the best friend
You can be,
So all around
Will surely see -

That you are good,
that you are kind.
and that, my friend,
Gives peace of mind.

Forgiven

When Momma folds her arms,
I know that she's upset.
And that my bad behavior,
is something I'll regret.

And when my Mom gets loud,
I know it's not a game.
And that for her distress,
I am surely to blame.

When Momma rolls her eyes,
She clearly is unhappy.
And if things don't improve,
She will soon get snappy.

And when Mom stomps her foot,
I know that I'm in trouble.
I hurry to my bedroom,
And get there on the double.

But when I see Mom smile,
I know I am forgiven.
And when she gives a hug,
Well, that feels just like Heaven.

Grow in Grace

You were made
to thrive and grow.
That is something
you should know.

Grow in beauty,
grow in grace.
Always keep
a happy face.

Let your light
shine bright each day,
To light all paths
along the way.

Know that you can
Help to make
The world be better –
For everyone's sake.

Let's Be Silly

I like to be silly –
but follow the rules.
'Cause if I'm not nice,
then it wouldn't be cool.

    Silly means laughter
    and silly means fun,
    But silly can never,
    ever hurt anyone.

        It can't be destructive
        or break anything,
        Because if it does –
        then that would be mean.

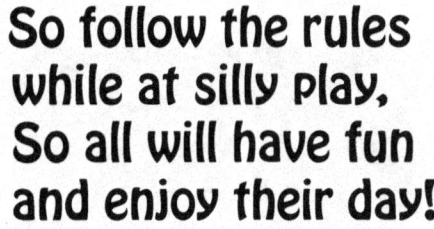

          So follow the rules
          while at silly play,
          So all will have fun
          and enjoy their day!

Upside Down Frown

Turn your frown upside down,
And choose to be happy today.
Turn your frown upside down,
And smile all the way.

Sometimes we feel bad and
It's hard to be glad,
But we should choose to be
Happy, not sad.

We won't let old sadness
Or sorry come 'round.
We can choose to just smile
And let joy abound.

So turn your frown upside down.
Now, that would be so ideal.
Make that frown go upside down,
And see how good you will feel.

Words of Comfort

Hold On

The storm clouds have all rolled away,
the sun is shining again.
There were days when I wasn't sure
I would make it to the end.

But here we are still standing strong,
and thankful for the sun.
Although our lives are not the same,
with this storm, we are done.

So thank you, God, for being there,
and giving strength to stand,
To make it through this trial in life –
by holding on to your hand.

Lead Me, Lord

Lead me to that solid rock,
that stands much taller than I,
for the strength of that solid rock
is what I need to get by.

Lead me not to the right or left,
but straight to the One who's above.
For I need a healthy dosage of
His mercy, grace and his love.

Measure out a healthy portion,
pour it on me this day,
so I may find the strength I need
to help me along the way.

May I never grow weary in giving,
may I never lose sight,
of all those that my life can bless,
if I choose to do what's right.

Rebuilding

This storm won't last forever,
The clouds will soon roll past.
The drops of rain that flood your life
Will never, ever last.

Flooded fields and trampled ground
may fill you with despair.
But take a big, deep, healthy breath
of freshly, renewed air.

You survived an awful storm,
And now it's time to build.
Time to restore what you've lost
And let your life be filled.

Filled with love, and filled with peace,
and letting go of loss.
Knowing that what now is gone
was left there at the cross.

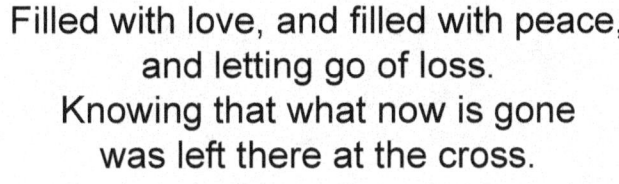

It's hard to know why storms may come
to fill our lives with strife.
But always good to know when past,
they benefit our life.

When triumphing within the storm
and standing strong throughout,
We'll find we stand much taller
while trusting God, no doubt.

The Storm

God can help you through this storm
Just trust in Him today.
Though the path seems long and hard,
He will lead the way.

Do not be so overwhelmed
That you become distressed.
Just keep your eyes upon the Lord,
And He will do the rest.

Let Him bring you safely through
And carry your big load.
One day soon you'll find your way,
He'll lead you down the road.

All bad storms will someday end
And life won't seem so bad,
The sun will once again shine down
And wash away the sad.

Trusting God

When everything around you
Seems to be going wrong,
Just look to God above
And try hard to be strong.

He knows what lies before you,
The road that you should take,
And He can help to guide you
With decisions you should make.

Though the path may not seem clear,
Or may be clouded by fog,
Just always put your trust in Him –
You can count on God.

His love will never fail you,
His peace will surely shine through,
Until the storm has gone away,
You'll find He's always true.

The Lord bless you and keep you;
The Lord make his face shine upon you
and be gracious to you:
The Lord turn his face toward you
and give you peace.

Numbers 6:24-26

For more words of encouragement,
check out Grandma Kitty's House
on Facebook and YouTube,

and also books by Kitty Kaye
on Amazon and Barnes and Noble.

CHILDREN'S BOOKS BY THE AUTHOR

After the Snowflakes *is a fully illustrated children's book about winter time activities. Each beautifully illustrated page shows a different event that celebrates fun things we can do after the snowflakes fall, including a few pages showing how different snowflakes could look. It ends with a playful poem about the uniqueness of snowflakes, encouraging the reader to get outside and enjoy the winter.*

ISBN: 978-1-7975666-4-1

Sunny Boy *is an illustrated children's book that discusses the role of the sun from an animated perpective. He starts to feel rejected when people don't appreciate him, but comes to realize the importance of the role he plays in the world around him. It is also a story of relationships and working together, as he forms a true friendship with Whispi the Cloud.*

ISBN: 978-1-7331639-2-7

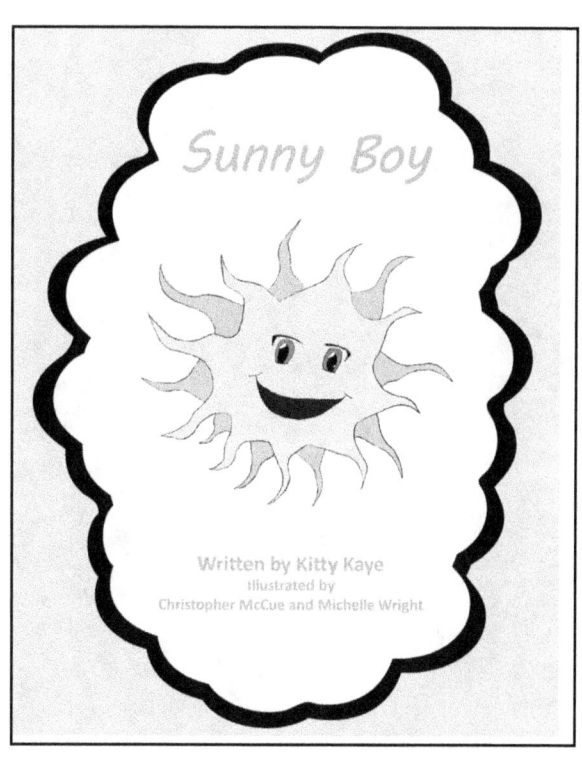